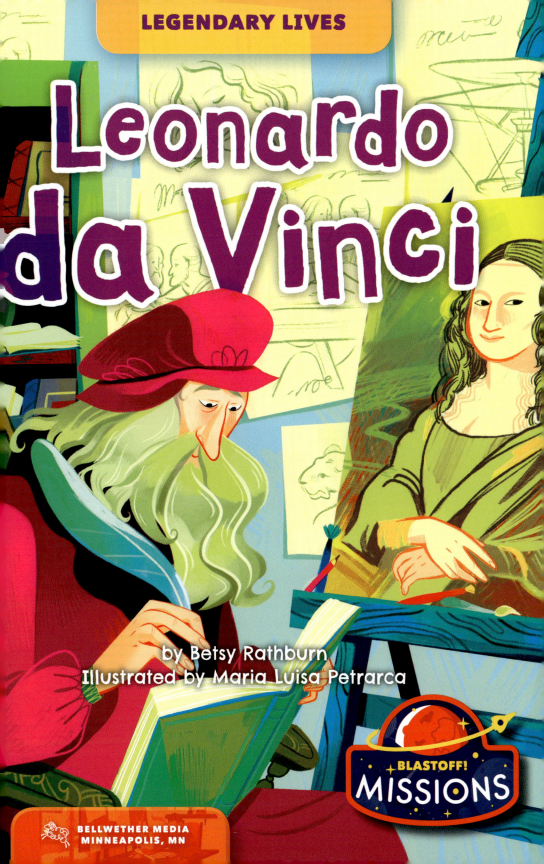

Blastoff! Missions takes you on a learning adventure! Colorful illustrations and exciting narratives highlight cool facts about our world and beyond. Read the mission goals and follow the narrative to gain knowledge, build reading skills, and have fun!

Traditional Nonfiction

Narrative Nonfiction

Blastoff! Universe

MISSION GOALS

> FIND YOUR SIGHT WORDS IN THE BOOK.

> LEARN ABOUT THE LIFE OF LEONARDO DA VINCI.

> LEARN ABOUT LEONARDO DA VINCI'S MOST FAMOUS PAINTINGS.

This edition first published in 2025 by Bellwether Media, Inc.

No part of this publication may be reproduced in whole or in part without written permission of the publisher. For information regarding permission, write to Bellwether Media, Inc., Attention: Permissions Department, 6012 Blue Circle Drive, Minnetonka, MN 55343.

Library of Congress Cataloging-in-Publication Data

LC record for Leonardo da Vinci available at: https://lccn.loc.gov/2024041927

Text copyright © 2025 by Bellwether Media, Inc. BLASTOFF! MISSIONS and associated logos are trademarks and/or registered trademarks of Bellwether Media, Inc.

Editor: Rebecca Sabelko   Designer: Andrea Schneider

Printed in the United States of America, North Mankato, MN.

This is **Blastoff Jimmy**! He is here to help you on your mission and share fun facts along the way!

Table of Contents

Meet Leonardo da Vinci 4
A Time to Learn 6
Renaissance Man 10
A Time to Teach 18
Glossary 22
To Learn More 23
Beyond the Mission 24
Index 24

ornithopter

Leonardo da Vinci is in his workshop. He draws ideas for his latest **invention**. The ornithopter is a flying machine. Leonardo imagines it will flap its wings like a bird!

It is the 1450s. Young Leonardo lives with his father in Vinci. This small town is near the important city of Florence, Italy.

Leonardo takes lessons in many areas. He learns reading, writing, and math.

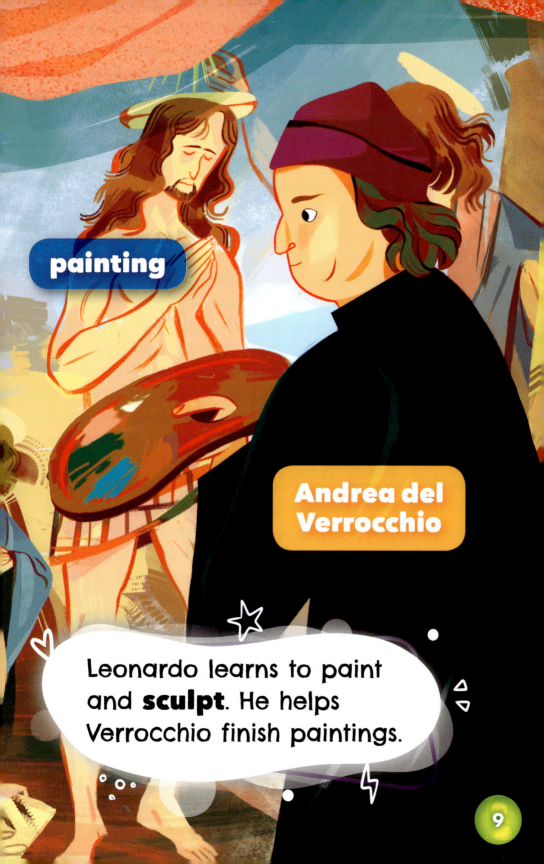

Renaissance Man

Leonardo now lives in the city of Milan. He works for the **duke** of the city.

He studies math and science. He becomes an **engineer**. He **designs** new machines.

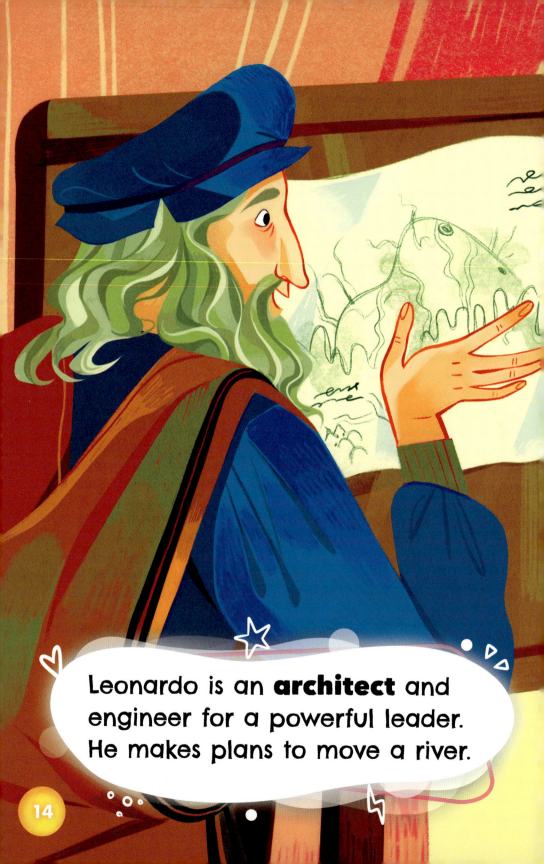

▶ **JIMMY SAYS** ◀
Mona Lisa is one of the most famous paintings in the world. Around 10 million people visit it in France each year!

Leonardo works on a new **portrait**. It is different from others of the **Renaissance**. The **subject** faces the viewer. Her hands show. *Mona Lisa* will **inspire** many artists!

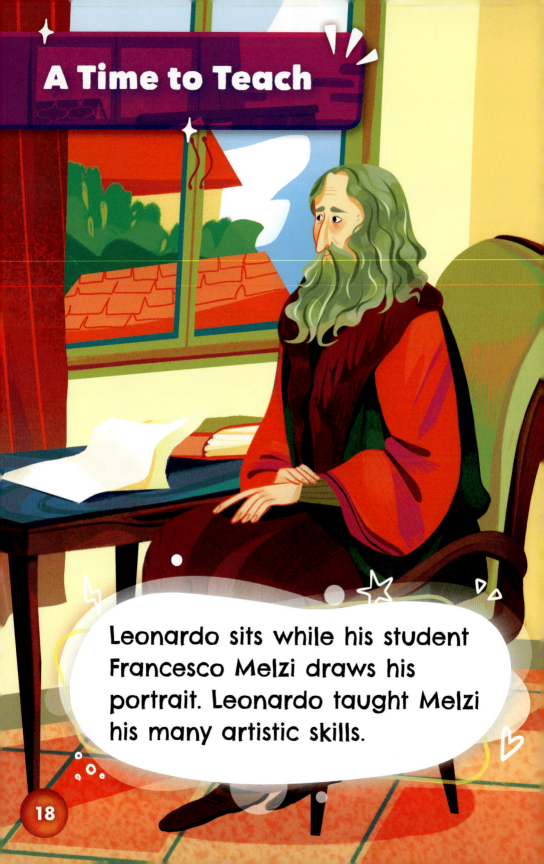

A Time to Teach

Leonardo sits while his student Francesco Melzi draws his portrait. Leonardo taught Melzi his many artistic skills.

Leonardo is famous throughout Europe. King Francis I invites him to France. Leonardo will spend the rest of his life here. In time, his work makes him famous around the world!

Leonardo da Vinci Profile

Born
April 15, 1452, in present-day Italy

Died
May 2, 1519

Accomplishments
Artist and scientist who painted some of the world's most famous paintings and designed many machines

Timeline

around 1467: Leonardo becomes an apprentice for Andrea del Verrocchio

1482: Leonardo moves to Milan to work for a duke and becomes an engineer

1498: Leonardo finishes painting *The Last Supper*

between 1503 and 1519: Leonardo paints *Mona Lisa*

between 1515 and 1518: Francesco Melzi draws the only known portrait of Leonardo

1516: Leonardo moves to France under the service of King Francis I

Glossary

apprentice—a person who works for and learns from another person

architect—a person who designs and plans buildings, bridges, and other things that are built

designs—thinks up and draws plans for something

duke—a man who rules over an area of land

engineer—a person who designs and builds machines

inspire—to give someone an idea about what to do or create

invention—something created for the first time

portrait—a painting, drawing, or photograph of a person

Renaissance—a period of growth in arts and writing from the 1300s to the 1600s in Europe

sculpt—to make objects out of stone, wood, or cla[y]

subject—a person or thing that is the focus of a work of art

To Learn More

AT THE LIBRARY

Krensky, Stephen. *Leonardo da Vinci*. New York, N.Y.: DK Publishing, 2020.

Meltzer, Brad. *I am Leonardo da Vinci*. New York, N.Y.: Dial Books for Young Readers, 2020.

Sabelko, Rebecca. *Italy*. Minneapolis, Minn.: Bellwether Media, 2023.

ON THE WEB

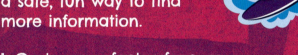

FACTSURFER

Factsurfer.com gives you a safe, fun way to find more information.

1. Go to www.factsurfer.com.

2. Enter "Leonardo da Vinci" into the search box and click 🔍.

3. Select your book cover to see a list of related content.

BEYOND THE MISSION

> WHAT FACT FROM THE BOOK DID YOU THINK WAS THE MOST INTERESTING?

> WHAT QUESTIONS WOULD YOU HAVE LIKED TO ASK LEONARDO DA VINCI?

> THINK ABOUT SOMETHING YOU WOULD LIKE TO INVENT. DRAW A DESIGN FOR IT.

Index

apprentice, 8
architect, 14
duke, 10, 13
engineer, 10, 14
Florence, Italy, 7
France, 17, 20
Francis I, 20
invention, 5
Last Supper, The, 13
machines, 5, 10
math, 7, 10
Melzi, Francesco, 18, 19
Milan, Italy, 10

Mona Lisa, 16, 17
ornithopter, 5
paint, 9, 13
paintings, 9, 13, 17
portrait, 16, 17, 18, 19
profile, 21
Renaissance, 17
science, 10
sculpt, 9
Verrocchio, Andrea del, 8, 9
Vinci, Italy, 7